Healthy Pastor–
Healthy Church!

Strengthening Pastoral Ministry In Your Congregation

S. Joan Hershey and Steve Clapp

**Published By
New Life Ministries & LifeQuest**

Healthy Pastor–Healthy Church! Strengthening Pastoral Ministry in Your Congregation

By S. Joan Hershey and Steve Clapp
Edited by Kristen Leverton Helbert

Copyright © 2002 by LifeQuest and New Life Ministries. Jointly published by LifeQuest and New Life Ministries. Contact: New Life Ministries Service Center, 6404 S. Calhoun Street, Fort Wayne, Indiana 46807. 1-800-774-3360.

All rights reserved. No portion of this book may be reproduced in any form or by any process or technique without the written consent of the publisher, except for brief quotations embodied in critical articles or reviews.

Biblical quotations, unless otherwise noted, are from the New Revised Standard Version of the Bible, copyrighted 1989 by the Division of Christian Education, National Council of Churches, and are used by permission. Some of the material in the chapter "Taking Care of Yourself–A Guide for Pastors" is adapted from *Creating Quality in Ministry* by Steve Clapp and Cindy Hollenberg [Andrew Center/LifeQuest, 1995, 1997].

> New Life Ministries extends appreciation to the General Board of the Church of the Brethren and to Mennonite Mutual Aid for grants which helped finance this publication.

We extend our thanks to the staff of Evangel Press for their high standards in the manufacturing of this resource. Ed Bontrager, Stan Dueck, Allen Hansell, Kristen Leverton Helbert, Celia King, Vyron L. Schmidt, and Glenn Timmons have all provided valuable guidance to this project.

ISBN 1-893270-06-8

Contents

Introduction   5
    Why we've written this booklet.

The Tension   8
    The difficulty of maintaining spiritual health in a performance-based culture.

Taking Care of Yourself–A Guide for Pastors   13
    Practical recommendations for physical, mental, social, and spiritual health.

Taking Care of the Pastor–A Guide for the Church Board, Executive Committee, Pastor-Parish Committee, and Other Official Groups   26
    The role of church leaders in keeping the pastor and the congregation healthy.

The Congregation–Supporting and Encouraging the Pastor   38
    Each person in the congregation has a role to play in helping the pastor be both healthy and effective.

When Change Comes   48
    Suggestions for handling pastoral transitions in healthy ways.

Discussion Questions   53
    Questions for a five-session study of this booklet.

Where to Learn More   56
    Other resources to help the pastor and the congregation.

If then there is any encouragement in Christ, any consolation from love, any sharing in the Spirit, any compassion and sympathy, make my joy complete: be of the same mind, having the same love, being in full accord and of one mind. Do nothing from selfish ambition or conceit; but in humility regard others as better than yourselves. Let each of you look not to your own interests, but to the interests of others. Let the same mind be in you that was in Christ Jesus.

Philippians 2:1-5

Introduction

On behalf of New Life Ministries we want to thank you for the concern about pastoral health and congregational health which brings you to these pages. Much thought and prayer have gone into this project, and we encourage you to read this booklet in that same spirit. We've endeavored to ground this booklet in:

- What Scripture teaches us about ministry and about the life of the church. Philippians 2:1-5 has been an important passage to us in the development of this resource.

- What has happened historically in the ministry of the Christian church.

- What we can learn from studies which have been conducted on congregational life.

We feel a little like the pastor who has done so much research and preparation that he could comfortably speak for an hour on Sunday morning but only has twenty minutes available! From the beginning of this project, we felt that a booklet would be more helpful than a book. Our hope is that this will be read not only by pastors but also by other church leaders and the congregation. Space does not permit us to address all the concerns we would have liked, but hopefully the booklet will serve as a catalyst for discussion and a renewed commitment to improving the health of the pastor and the congregation.

Steve Clapp, one of the authors of this booklet, speaking at a conference of clergy from many different denominations, asked those who were present to respond anonymously on notecards to five questions:

1. Have you had times when the pressures of ministry seriously harmed your physical health? **48% said yes.**

2. Have you had times when the pressures of ministry seriously harmed your mental health? **64% said yes.**

3. Have you had times when the pressures of ministry seriously harmed your spiritual health? **74% said yes.**

4. Have you seriously considered leaving the ministry? **71% said yes.**

5. Are there times when your ministry is harmed because you are not in the best physical, mental, or spiritual health? **91% said yes.**

Does this mean we are facing a new epidemic in terms of the health of clergy? Not necessarily. Clergy have always faced significant stress because of the particular work to which they are called, and we do not know what the results of a similar survey would have been in the time of the apostle Paul!

But we are certainly living in a time when there are many pressures on clergy, and we have not always provided strong support structures. Effective pastors are critical to churches, but–
  Some are not effective.
    Some are not healthy.
      Some are not effective or healthy.
And some very gifted pastors burn out on the ministry and leave permanently.

Many clergy have graduated from both college and seminary and are working as full-time professionals. We also recognize that there are large numbers of clergy who have received their training in other ways. With many small congregations unable to afford a full-time pastor, bivocational clergy play an increasingly important role. Some traditions have a plural (sometimes called free) ministry in which pastors serve without salary. Virtually all denominations have experienced an increase in the number of persons choosing ministry as a second career.

The challenges of ministry depend not only on the background and training of the pastor but also on the nature of the congregation and of the community which it serves. The stress which affects a pastor on the staff of a 5,000 member congregation in a suburban setting can differ significantly from that of a part-time pastor serving a congregation of 50 in a rural community. Each situation brings unique challenges, pressures, and rewards.

In a publication of this size, it is impossible to provide a comprehensive discussion of every issue affecting the health of

Strengthening Pastoral Ministry *Page 7*

every pastor. We have focused on those issues which seem to us to affect the greatest number of pastors and congregations.

We do not intend to minimize the reality of the priesthood of all believers–in fact, we hope that the pages which follow will make clear how important the ministry of every member of the congregation is. Our focus within these pages, however, is on the health of clergy and how that relates to the health of the congregation.

One reader of an early draft of this manuscript raised some astute questions: "What happens when a healthy pastor comes to a sick congregation? Will the pastor be able to maintain his or her own health and improve the congregation? Or will the pastor become sick under the influence of the church?" Obviously we hope the pastor stays healthy and is a positive influence on the church, but there are situations in which that can be very difficult. We recognize that the health of the pastor is only one of many issues affecting the health of the congregation. If pastors can stay healthy, they will be a positive influence on others even in difficult situations. There are also times when both the pastor and the church must recognize that the match between them is not right. We address that to a limited extent in our concluding chapter *When Change Comes*.

This booklet will be of limited use if only read by pastors. It should certainly be read by Pastor Parish, Staff Relations, Ministerial, or Executive Committees–those groups charged with the support and supervision of the pastor and his or her work. It should also be studied by elders, leadership teams, and church boards. In fact our hope is that the whole congregation will want to read the booklet and become part of the supportive network that ensures a healthy pastor.

Three chapters are addressed to specific audiences: to pastors, to supervising/supporting groups, and to congregations. A few concepts are intentionally repeated in those chapters. We hope that each person receiving this booklet will read it from cover-to-cover, but we recognize that busy people sometimes read first what is most directly addressed to them.

We would like to hear about your experiences using this booklet and can be reached through New Life Ministries or LifeQuest at the address on page 2.

Joan and Steve

The Tension

As the spring of 1992 drew to a close, I began a terrifying descent into a debilitating dark night. Having spent two decades in Christian ministry, I was reaping an unpleasant harvest gathered from years of overwork and a performance-based approach to ministry. What began as ever increasing seasons of anxiety ultimately lead to deep depression and a frightening bout of agoraphobia [fear of open or public places]. I felt terribly lost and without help or hope.

Those words of Terry Wardle, from his book *The Soul's Journey* [p. 15], describe the trap into which some pastors fall. It's very easy for a pastor who is deeply dedicated to the well-being of the congregation to get caught in a tension between the needs of the church and his or her own needs as a human being.

Every church has deep needs—both the people who participate in the church and the church as an organization. Many mainline Protestant and Anabaptist churches have experienced significant decline over the last two or three decades, and congregational morale is often low in the face of such losses. Other churches have had the good fortune to experience significant growth but also face the challenges of meeting the needs of a diverse membership and continually integrating new people into the life of the church.

Church members and constituents, pastors, and denominational leaders know that effective pastors make a difference! There is a growing body of evidence that some churches which are in decline have not staffed for growth. Many denominations are dealing with a declining supply of clergy precisely when they are most needed!

The professional ministry has borrowed from other disciplines; and we frequently apply terms like goals, objectives, targets, and performance-based evaluation to the work of clergy. Certainly pastoral effectiveness and accountability are very important to the life of the church. Yet it's easy for clergy to get caught in a performance-based life, in which they are driven by the same forces that drive the majority of people in our culture of addiction to work and achievement. When that happens:

>Pastors lose their way,
>>their health,
>>>their loved ones,
>>>>and their effectiveness.

As important as effectiveness may be, it cannot be permitted to be the only goal of pastoral ministry. Allen Hansell reminds us that:

> *Ministerial leadership is more than a profession or a career. Ministry is a vocation, a calling by God and the church. It is a call to go where God defines the need and provides the message. The need is next door and it is also global.*
> [**Messenger** article, Jan/Feb 2001, p. 27]

Faithfulness to the call and direction of God should be in all of our hearts, and God does not intend to burn us out!

Expectations of the pastor and of the congregation are sometimes in conflict. For example:

Some Pastors Expect	**Some Congregations Expect**
Members should share in the provision of pastoral care	Pastors should do all of the hospital visitation
I am a spiritual leader; people should respect my authority	Pastors should say what I want to hear
Members will come to me with any news	Pastors should be involved and know what is happening
Members will help me understand the systems and traditions of the church	Pastors will automatically understand the way our church operates

When the pastor and the congregation are not clear about mutual expectations, both can become frustrated. Most congregations do not have a single set of expectations of the pastor. What people want in terms of worship leadership, sermon content, pastoral care, and even leadership style can vary significantly. Many tensions in recent years have related to the service of worship, with some people clinging to traditional styles, while others are hungry for more contemporary or alternative approaches.

Some church members desperately want the church to avoid change, to be a safe harbor in the midst of a rapidly changing world. Others are almost desperate for the church to be transformed. In *Change and the Established Congregation*, Paul Mundey quotes one pastor who describes what many feel:

> It's like I'm pastoring two different congregations. . . . At times it literally seems impossible to successfully pastor both congregations at the same time. Their expectations are so different. And the issue of change is the core one. [p. 13]

Pastors who give the best leadership in the midst of the tensions and pressures of congregational life are ones who are physically, mentally, and spiritually healthy. They have the perspective and the spiritual reserves to deal with the inevitable tensions without becoming burned out. They are able to celebrate success, but they are also able to rebound from failure and frustration.

Healthy Pastors Make a Difference

The pastor must take the primary responsibility for his or her personal health and well-being, but no pastor can be successful in that effort without the help and support of church leaders and most of the congregation. None of us as individuals, whether pastors or church members, can resolve all the tensions that are part of the life of the church in our time. But all of us can work at healthier attitudes and at creating a climate in which ministry can flourish. There are many examples around North America of the difference that healthy, effective pastors can make. For example:

- A pastor of a church which had resisted change in worship for years instituted a dialogue between younger and older members of the congregation with the result that a new blended worship service gained acceptance.

- A new youth pastor of a church which had very few young people developed a creative program of street hockey which revitalized the youth program and much of the church as well.

- A pastor who had recovered from a heart attack resolved to live a less stressful life and enlisted the help of the entire congregation in that process. He cut his work week from eighty-five hours to forty-five hours, and the church began to grow!

- A church whose pastor had never taken more than a week of vacation decided to pay the expenses for a month's vacation for the pastor and the pastor's family. The pastor, who had been considering leaving the ministry, returned from the vacation with new appreciation for the church and for the ministry.

- A church which had been in decline for years recognized that the pastor was too overloaded to give leadership to outreach efforts. The church instituted a Stephen's Ministry program to involve lay leadership in providing some pastoral care. Then the church decided to add another full-time pastor with members doing "extra mile" giving as though contributing to a building fund. The church became filled with new life and began to grow.

- A bivocational pastor of a small congregation felt drained by the responsibility of providing pastoral care and doing church administration at the end of long days of secular work. The church developed a spiritual gifts system that matched members with their gifts and areas of need in the congregation. The pastor's workload went down, and the church's energy went up.

- The senior pastor of a 4,500 member congregation showed great energy in public but felt privately exhausted after fifteen years of leadership. He wanted to retire but was afraid that the church would suffer tremendous membership losses when he did so. He shared his heart with the elders of the church who helped develop a succession plan so there could be a smooth transition and less pressure.

- A pastor who felt burned out and felt that his leadership was no longer effective enlisted four members of the church as a Pastoral Support Group. The four people prayed for the pastor each day and met with the pastor once a week for prayer and Bible study on the nature of ministry. The pastor's personal life was renewed, and the four members of the Pastoral Support Group became a strong force for renewal in the life of the church.

- A pastor who felt drained and low on enthusiasm took a short sabbatical, only two months, and used it to work in a poverty-stricken neighborhood a thousand miles from her congregation. Many thought this a very unrestful way to spend a sabbatical, but the pastor found her faith and her energy renewed. When she returned to the parish, she shared so much enthusiasm for the difference that could be made in that distant neighborhood that twenty people went there with her the following year. That became the basis for a renewal of the whole church.

What can you do, as a pastor, as a church leader, or as a member of the congregation, to nurture the kind of pastoral health that results in congregational health? How do we find balance? How do we open ourselves fully to God's grace and help in the midst of the tensions that exist in congregational life? Keep reading!

Taking Care of Yourself–
A Guide for Pastors

Taking Care of Yourself

1. Nurture your own spiritual life or your perspective on everything else will be distorted. Authors, speakers, denominational executives, and counselors all emphasize the importance of developing the spiritual life; and virtually everyone reading these words would be in agreement that this is a priority in the life of church professionals and of all people who take their faith seriously. But how many of us really do it on a consistent basis? Consider these questions:

- Do you have a devotional time built into each day?
- Do you take an annual spiritual retreat?
- In the depths of your heart, do you believe God has the power to solve your problems?
- What part does listening to God play in your life?
- Do you feel God leading you in the major decisions of your life?

Time spent in sermon and teaching preparation certainly may help your spiritual life, but it is not the same as time reserved for the development of your relationship with God through prayer, solitude, and devotional reading.

The cultivation of a close, intimate relationship with God fails to happen for many of us, regardless of occupation, not out of a lack of a desire but out of the pressures of daily life. Ministers, who deal routinely with the problems of others, may find it especially difficult to consistently protect devotional time. The pastor of one of the largest congregations in the country shared with Steve Clapp:

> *I feel good about my ministry and my life most of the time, but I never stop running. I'm charging ahead*

> from the moment my alarm goes off at 5 a.m. until I literally crash into bed at 11 p.m.–well, 11 p.m. when I'm lucky. Sometimes it's later. I follow the principles in Stephen Covey's **First Things First**; and most of the time, I don't neglect my family. But my own devotional life, that's another matter. I have a deep spiritual life in the sense that I pray almost continually and feel God's presence with me. But I don't often sit still long enough for there to be the possibility of God speaking to me. That probably harms my leadership, but it primarily harms my faith.

And those same feelings are experienced by many pastors of churches of all sizes. Bivocational pastors find themselves juggling the responsibilities of two careers in addition to family, community, and personal needs. People who are enrolled in Bible college or seminary and also pastoring can feel immense pressure. The suggestions offered in this chapter can help in protecting time to cultivate the spiritual life; but it is also crucial to make the personal choice that time for this is of paramount importance, no matter how great the other demands.

2. Keep physically fit but avoid conditioning binges. If you don't keep physically fit, you won't have the needed energy to be productive at work or in your personal life. Poor physical conditioning can also keep you from living as long a life as is your potential. A firm commitment to a regular exercise program, to a healthy diet, and to the avoidance of habits which are detrimental to your overall well-being can add pleasure, years, and productivity to your life.

Some of us have spent years getting out of shape. A decision to reverse that in a single week or month generally results in a short-term conditioning binge which leaves one exhausted, sore, and disillusioned with fitness programs. If you spent years getting out of shape, accept the fact that you need to get back into shape gradually. Whether your own preferred habit is a certain amount of exercise five days a week, three days a week, or another frequency, something on a regular basis is the way to go. The better your physical condition, the more energy you will have for mental and spiritual development. Do a quick evaluation using this checklist:

_____ I exercise on a regular basis (at least three days a week).
_____ I eat breakfast each morning.
_____ I am reasonably consistent in the time that I eat my meals and in the amount I eat.

_____ I avoid excessive fat and sugar in my diet.
_____ I get sufficient vitamins and minerals from my diet or take an appropriate supplement.
_____ I get enough sleep each night that waking in the morning isn't overly difficult, and I don't have to fight sleep while driving or sitting in meetings.
_____ I don't smoke.
_____ I drink alcoholic beverages in moderation or not at all.
_____ I take good care of my teeth.
_____ I have regular eye examinations including testing for glaucoma.
_____ I get regular examinations from a dentist and a physician who understand prevention as well as cure.
_____ I don't procrastinate about seeing a doctor or dentist when I have symptoms that obviously need attention.

3. Plan your vacation well in advance and see that pastoral coverage is arranged, or you aren't likely to have a vacation! Most denominational policies and congregational employment contracts include vacation time for clergy and other church staff members. Generally speaking, the church board or personnel committee has responsibility for providing pulpit and pastoral coverage during that period of time. Staff members who fail to take initiative in protecting the time for vacation, however, will often have difficulty getting away. The calendar fills quickly, and pulpit supply isn't always an easy matter.

Bivocational and other part-time clergy need vacation time just as much as full-time clergy. Persons juggling a secular job as well as a pastoral position generally work large numbers of hours and deal with multiple pressures. Vacation can bring needed relaxation and perspective. Those in the plural or free ministry, who serve without salary, also need periods of time without church responsibilities.

Some pastors feel guilty about taking vacation time–some work always seems to go undone, and there are almost always pastoral care concerns. Failing to take that time, however, generally results in frustration and stress which lowers the quality of the ministry one performs. There is an old joke which still has truth. A congregational member said to the pastor, "I don't see why you get four weeks of vacation a year. That's a lot of time, and Sunday is the only day you really work anyway."

The pastor responded, "If I'm doing a good job, then I deserve the time free. If I'm doing a bad job, then the congregation deserves the time free from me. Either way, it's a good idea. Besides, if you figure I'm only working one day a week, then the vacation is only for four days."

4. Keep on learning! The pace of change in today's society is extremely fast. Indeed, the rate of change itself seems to keep increasing! Our time has been referred to as the "Information Age," and that seems an accurate description. New information keeps being made available, and the growth of the Internet has both overwhelmed and fascinated most of us. The tragic events of September 11, 2001 caused many pastors to seek new information on the Islamic faith and on dealing with fear and anxiety.

It's important to maintain a commitment to continuing education opportunities and to reading and study which are sources of new information, new perspectives, and renewal. Warren Bennis and Burt Nanus studied the background and styles of ninety top leaders from a variety of fields. They found that leaders were distinguished from followers largely by the extent to which they kept developing and cultivating their skills and knowledge [shared by Chuck Swindoll in *Strengthening Your Grip*]. People who are successful are serious about being lifelong learners and make that one of their priorities. This kind of learning can take place in many ways:

- Through daily reading and study of professional journals and books.
- Through study opportunities available on the web.
- Through workshops and seminars offered by the denomination and other organizations.
- Through formal continuing education opportunities offered by seminaries, universities, and denominational agencies.
- Through the development of a Pastoral Support Group for professional care and critique. This might be a group of clergy from your own denomination who live in reasonable proximity, a group of clergy from a variety of denominations, or a carefully chosen group of people from your own congregation.

Recognize the reality, however, that you cannot in a single year intensively study every new trend in theology, biblical studies, church history, administration, missions, evangelism, worship, stewardship, Christian education, and youth work. That's asking the impossible of yourself! Determine what areas are most important for your own ministry and the ministry of your congregation. Over a period of four or five years, you can achieve a greater amount of balance in your continuing education than in any one year. This perspective is especially important for bivocational clergy who may be working to keep current in two fields.

5. Create a personal support system for yourself. This certainly can include the kind of Pastoral Support Group mentioned under number four. Most of us need a reasonably broad support system which may include:

- Your spouse and children, who need to understand your work and the pressures which are part of it. While there are certainly some confidences from counseling which you keep only to yourself, your family will usually benefit from being aware of what is happening in your professional life. This is particularly true for your spouse but can also be true for your children, depending on their ages. Knowing the concerns which weigh on you can help them be part of your support structure and will also help them understand you better. You, of course, also want to be a supportive presence in their lives, recognizing that they experience pressures of their own.

- You may choose another pastor to be a mentor to you. This could be a retired pastor living nearby. With the ease of communication through e-mail and the telephone, it is also possible for such a relationship to be cultivated with a pastor who lives at a distance.

- Select a Prayer Group in your church which includes three or four members who have helpful perspectives on the life of the church and whom you know are personally supportive of you. Ask them to pray for you daily and to have breakfast with you weekly. Have a time of prayer when you meet together, share the concerns which are weighing on you, and invite them to share anything which they feel you should be aware of in the life of the church.

Be sure to give to some of those in your support system the privilege to offer constructive criticism. You obviously want them to be supportive of your ministry, but that supportiveness may sometimes need to take the form of pointing out an area of concern for you.

It's especially important to be aware of co-dependency and self-differentiation issues in ministry. It's very easy for a pastor and significant people in a congregation to become trapped in unhealthy relationships which harm the pastor and the church. The need for approval and the need for control can both cause us to relate in ways which are not healthy. Having people who will speak frankly to you can spare both you and the church considerable pain.

Pastors sometimes find themselves serving churches which have tremendous resistance to change and to the pastor's efforts at providing leadership. When working in such situations, pastors almost desperately need a support system which will provide honest feedback. Is the pastor pushing too hard or in ineffective ways? Does the congregation have major systemic problems which are not likely to be changed by the pastor? Is the match between the pastor and the congregation a poor one? At what point should the pastor attempt to change his or her style of leadership? At what point should the pastor consider moving to another congregation? Struggling with such difficult questions becomes much easier with the support, love, and honest feedback of others.

Organizing for Work and Health

6. Keep a notecard with you which lists your mission or vision and most important goals or priorities. If you have a personal mission or vision statement, then that belongs on the card. You also want to carry whatever comparable statement the congregation may have developed. Concisely list the top priorities or goals for the year ahead for yourself and for the church. (Consider developing a personal mission statement if you do not have one. A family mission statement can also be a great help, but it should not replace your own.) The personal mission or vision statement for a bivocational pastor may include goals or priorities related to the pastoral calling and to secular work.

Don't carry the notecard inside a calendar or wallet. Keep it separate, so that you will have to handle it at least twice a day (once when getting dressed and once when getting ready for bed). Mission or vision statements can make a tremendous difference in our lives, but only to the extent that those truly become the focus of our effort. Use what you've written on the card as a test of the decisions which you must make during the day. Looking at the card on a regular basis can keep you aware of your commitment to writing a book, developing a contemporary service, or launching a new evangelistic outreach into the neighborhood around your congregation.

Strengthening Pastoral Ministry

7. Learn to set priorities for both the long term and for a week at a time–making the week the basic unit of planning. There are two traps in planning which can be limiting:

- Planning only one day at a time makes it difficult to accomplish major projects or changes. The priorities of the day can completely push aside long-term planning, sermon preparation, the physical fitness program you keep wanting to begin, and your intentions to design an improved stewardship campaign. Blocking off time several weeks or even months in advance for vacations, seminars, and work on major projects is a very wise strategy.

- Making specific plans too far in advance, however, invites frustration because so many things happen which are beyond one's control. Those who lay out in great detail how a day of work will be spent three weeks in the future are likely to be frustrated. Special meetings get called, people are hospitalized, family crises erupt, and deaths generally come with no warning at all.

Henri J. M. Nouwen writes in his book *In the Name of Jesus–Reflections on Christian Leadership*: "God is a God of the present and reveals to those who are willing to listen carefully to the moment in which they live the steps they are to take toward the future" [pp.3-4]. God will help us, in the present, to make plans for the future–but those plans are always going to be subject to change! We need to blend the ability to plan with an openness to God's continuing direction in the present.

8. Keep a current and accurate list of "tasks to be done" in ONE PLACE! That place may be in a small spiral notebook, in a folder on your desk, on index cards that you keep in your pocket, in a larger spiral notebook that you keep on your desk or in your briefcase, or in a similar format. The list needs to be in a single place, and it needs to be accessible to you almost all the time, so that you can keep it current. Those who are into technology may want to keep it on computer.

9. Keep a single calendar, and keep it up to date. Most of us are not capable of keeping more than a single calendar current on a continuing basis. We may like the idea of having a calendar at the office, at the home, and in the pocket; but all three are almost never going to be current at the same time. Keep a single calendar to manage your work, but photocopy pages from it when appropriate to share with your family and the church office. You may find that maintaining a calendar on your computer is a very easy way to keep current and that you can readily make copies for your secretary and family. For those comfortable with them, Palm Pilots and similar devices are a wonderful innovation (as long as you have backup)!

You may wish to give your secretary certain blocks of time for which it is all right to make appointments for you, but don't give that person control over your entire schedule. Also be sure that you honor those blocks of time reserved for your family, for exercise, and for devotions.

10. Decide on a reasonable amount of time to work each week, and discipline yourself to stay within that amount unless you are faced with multiple emergencies. Remember, as a church staff member, that lay persons are generally working at least forty hour weeks (either as a paid employee or in the home) and then donating additional time to the congregation. Thus full-time church professionals sometimes find that forty hours a week just isn't enough time. Lay persons are not wrong in expecting that full-time clergy will work something over forty hours a week given the reality that lay persons are donating so much of their own time to the congregation. You have to decide for yourself what is reasonable.

From interviews with lay persons of many different denominations over the years, it appears clear to us that very few expect church staff members to work more than fifty to sixty hours a week. Some active lay persons are disappointed if full-time church professionals, other than custodial or secretarial staff, work only forty hours a week, but their expectations are not for seventy, eighty, and ninety hour weeks. In fact, most people feel that the quality of a person's work is impaired if that person does not have enough personal time and does not get enough rest. We live in a culture in which addiction to work and productivity is commonplace, and clergy need to model lives which are balanced. A forty hour week may not be realistic, but more than fifty-five hours a week is not likely to be healthy.

If you are a bivocational pastor or other part-time church employee, then the decision-making can be especially difficult. Churches are notoriously guilty of expecting more from part-time employees than is fair. If the church has not been clear with you about how many hours a week of work are expected, then ask questions until you gain that clarity. If your job has been expressed as quarter time, one-third time, half time, or a similar fraction, think of that as half (or a third or. . .) of a fifty hour week. That approach eliminates any doubt about whether or not you are earning your keep.

Full-time clergy may find it helpful to think of the week in terms of twenty-one blocks of time, with each morning, afternoon, and evening representing a separate block. If you use this approach, adjust your schedule each week so that you are not working more than fourteen or fifteen of those blocks. This will generally result in your working fifty to sixty hours a week and may be an easier approach to thinking about your time. Here is an example:

	Monday	Tuesday	Wednesday	Thursday	Friday	Saturday	Sunday
Morning	xxxx	xxxx	xxxx		xxxx		xxxx
Afternoon	xxxx	xxxx	xxxx	xxxx	xxxx		xxxx
Evening			xxxx	xxxx			xxxx

11. Be open and direct in speaking with church leaders about your needs and about the pressures of ministry. Many who enter the ministry take their calling so seriously that they are reluctant to bring up financial matters or work load issues with the church. Church leaders can be very intelligent and committed people who appreciate your ministry and still not understand the financial problems and the stress that often accompany a pastor's work. They need your help in understanding your work and your needs.

Almost all churches have a committee or board which is responsible for the supervision and support of the pastor. Adopt a style of openness and honesty in your conversations with that group. If you feel that you are underpaid, tell them. If you are having problems paying for medical and dental care with the existing health insurance provided, tell them. If you are concerned that the retirement benefits provided are not adequate, tell them. If you are working too many hours and need guidance in deciding how to set priorities, tell them. If there are congregational expectations of you which are unfair and you need help in interpreting your work, tell them.

Very few of us respond favorably to demands or expressions of anger, but almost all of us respond positively when others share concerns openly. You'll find that the committee or board with which you work will be far more supportive of you when helped to understand your concerns and needs.

Spiritual Gifts Assessment

Ministry can almost always be strengthened through knowledge of the spiritual gifts which one possesses. Many different instruments have been developed to help identify spiritual gifts. New Life Ministries and Christian Community offer one in the publication *Preaching, Planning, and Plumbing*; and other good spiritual gift inventories are available.

Operating without an awareness of the spiritual gifts you have been given can result in frustration and burnout! The frustration affects both you and the congregation you are serving. A spiritual gifts inventory should be taken at least every five years because our gifts may change as we mature spiritually.

The congregation has a responsibility to compliment your ministry by calling persons with gifts that are not your highest to work in supportive ways. For example, if administration is not one of your gifts, a recognition of that can be helpful to both you and the congregation. There are others with that gift who can give you help in administrative areas. Understanding your spiritual gifts can also be very important when consideration is being given to employing additional ministerial staff. Rather than hiring someone with the same spiritual gifts you possess, seek a person whose gifts will compliment yours.

An understanding of spiritual gifts by the congregation as a whole can open up exciting possibilities for ministry. Research by Christian Community, Natural Church Development, and others confirms the reality that growing, healthy churches help church members identify their own spiritual gifts and the ministries to which they are called. Thus members of the church are not viewed as "helpers" to carry out a ministry that has been defined by the denomination, the pastor, or even a small group of church leaders. Rather, each person in the church is viewed as possessing valuable gifts for ministry. The ministry of the church as a whole grows out of the particular spiritual gifts which are held by people in the congregation. The results can be exciting–and truly make the pastor's role one of leading and enabling the ministry of others.

> The *Personal Development Inventory* which appears on the next page can be a useful tool in thinking about your overall health and your ministry. It is modified from one by Steven L. Ogne and Thomas P. Nebel and is used with the permission of CoachNet.

Personal Development Inventory for Clergy

Score yourself from one to five on the following, with five being best.

___ 1. I understand and can verbalize my personal mission and calling.
___ 2. (If married) My spouse and I agree that our personal and family life is in balance.
___ 3. I have a personal growth plan, including mental, physical, spiritual, and ministry goals.
___ 4. I feel fulfilled in my roles at home.
___ 5. I feel fulfilled in my ministry roles.
___ 6. I feel that I spend the needed time with my family.
___ 7. I feel that I take good care of my physical health.
___ 8. I feel that I take good care of my spiritual health.
___ 9. I feel that I have stayed on top of new information and strategies which can help my ministry.
___ 10. My ministry assignments are consistent with my God-given gifts for ministry.
___ 11. I am regularly involved in professional growth and learning opportunities.
___ 12. I have identified mentors in life and ministry.
___ 13. I am currently mentoring others.
___ 14. I am accountable to others for my personal life and ministry.
___ 15. I relate to others in such a way that they can comfortably share suggestions and positive criticism with me.
___ 16. I use a calendar, lists, and other tools in ways that keep me organized and on top of my ministry.
___ 17. I feel that I am working about the right number of hours and that I am being as effective as possible during that time.
___ 18. I feel that I protect enough time for my family and for personal relaxation.
___ 19. I have been able to avoid becoming co-dependent or developing other unhealthy relationships with people in the church.
___ 20. I feel, overall, that my life flows consistently with my understanding of God's calling.

Bivocational Clergy

In his insightful book *Discontinuity and Hope*, Lyle Schaller reminds us that there has been a "gradual shrinkage in the number of congregations averaging fewer than a hundred at worship that can both economically afford and also justify in terms of a challenging work load, a full-time and fully credentialed resident pastor" [p. 117]. There are now an estimated 105,000 bivocational ministers, retired ministers, and lay persons serving small churches.

Some of the pastors reading this booklet will be bivocational, and some of the congregational members reading this booklet are being served by bivocational pastors. It is likely that the number of pastors in this category will increase in the years ahead. References to bivocational ministry are made in relevant places throughout this publication, but it also seems appropriate to say a few things about the nature of this approach to ministry.

The Brethren Academy for Ministerial Leadership and Christian Community did a study on bivocational ministry which showed that most bivocational pastors are happy in their work–and that their congregations feel well served. The study showed:

- Bivocational pastors have a wide range of secular careers which provide a good part of their financial support. Some are in fields such as medicine, social work, education, and banking. Others are electricians, plumbers, and farmers.

- The success of bivocational clergy in managing both positions depends in good measure on the type of secular career chosen. Bivocational respondents overwhelmingly favored being self-employed as the best option for a complementary vocation with ministry, simply due to the fact that self-employment is flexible enough to allow schedule changes with little notice. Those who work for others reported the least tension when their secular employers were made aware of the nature of their work as pastor–and when church members understood the limitations imposed by the secular employment. Open, frank communication reduces stress and sometimes can result in creative solutions to problems.

- Some bivocational ministers received their training and education for both occupations at about the same time. The majority, however, decided to become employed in a bivocational capacity after they had completed college or other training for secular employment. Sixty-six percent stated that their first employment was not as a minister, 26% were employed in the ministerial position first, and only 8% started both at the same time.

- Whether or not a minister was employed in a secular position first does have some impact on the reasons for being bivocational. Although financial need was cited as an important reason for having two vocations by both groups, those who chose a secular job after they were already in ministry were more likely to list need for greater income as an incentive than those who chose ministry after their secular occupation.

- Forty-eight percent of those who indicated that they were bivocational pastors work full-time in their non-ministerial position, and 32% work part-time in that position. The others experienced a wider range of hours in the non-ministerial position, and a few were retired from their secular work though still see themselves as bivocational. Time management becomes an especially important skill for the bivocational minister.

- Only 35% of the bivocational pastors surveyed had received a traditional seminary degree. The average number of years spent training for ministry (4 years) was very similar to the average number of years spent training for the non-ministerial position (3.45 years). The ministerial training, however, was more likely to have been through undergraduate study or a denominational guided study program than through graduate level seminary training. Bivocational pastors, on the whole, felt that continuing education was *very important* to their ministry.

- Most bivocational pastors are serving small churches. The fact that our society often equates "large" with "good" causes some frustrations for those pastors and their churches. It's easy for the congregation to have low self-esteem and for the pastor to feel frustrated by inability to achieve significant growth. It's important for the pastor and the church to have healthy dialogue about what needs to happen and about what can realistically be expected. Many small congregations have vital, focused ministries and much to celebrate!

Taking Care of the Pastor—
A Guide for the Church Board, Executive Committee, Pastor-Parish Committee, and Other Official Groups

1. Clarify goals and expectations with the pastor and with other professional staff. This may not mean a rigid job description. The trend in many businesses now is to develop a job description which fits on a single page and recognizes that needs are continually changing. Extremely detailed job descriptions can be unrealistic and frustrating. The job description shouldn't attempt to tell the pastor how to do his or her job but should convey what is most important.

While there are areas in which clearly measurable expectations can be helpful, the quality of ministry is not always easily quantified. Certainly it can be helpful for a pastor to have a goal of ten visits in homes each week, but the quality of what happens in those visits is not so easy to measure. It can be helpful to clearly state that the pastor is responsible for worship services forty-five weeks of the year (with the other weeks providing for vacation time, continuing education time, and special emphases with outside speakers); but the quality of those services is of greater importance to the congregation than whether the actual number led by the pastor is a couple more or less than the agreed amount. It's good to make clear that the pastor is expected to attend board meetings except while on vacation, but the worth of the guidance given by the pastor at those meetings is not readily converted to numbers or a checklist.

Note the discussion about the pastor's time and schedule shared in the previous chapter. While most full-time pastors work more than forty hours a week, very few pastors are going to function effectively when they start working more than fifty-five hours a week. If church leaders continually convey impatience to the pastor about needs which are not being met, it's easy for the minister to work an excessive number of hours which will interfere with his or her health and effectiveness.

Churches served by bivocational and other part-time pastors need to be just as sensitive to issues of the pastor's time and health as those served by full-time clergy. Some bivocational pastors are carrying an enormous load and need the support of church leaders in setting realistic expectations and boundaries. Congregations of all sizes have an unfortunate tendency to take advantage of part-time staff, who often work far more hours than the number for which they are compensated. The work load of the church shouldn't get handled by taking advantage of staff.

There are instances in which part-time staff members genuinely want to work more hours than the number for which they are compensated. When that is the case, the extra work needs to be accepted by the congregation with gratitude *as a gift* and should not be permitted to become the expectation for the future.

Churches which are served by plural or free ministers, who do not receive financial compensation, still need to be in dialogue with the pastor or pastors about their work loads. Some congregations utilizing a free ministry tradition have sufficient free (volunteer) pastors that the work load on any one person is not excessive. There are other situations in which the work load on one or two persons becomes excessive, leading to the same kind of burn-out as salaried clergy can experience.

Talk realistically and frankly with the pastor about how many hours he or she is generally working in a week. If that number is excessive, identify ways to help with the work load. Consider doing an exercise like the one on the next page as a way of opening discussion on priorities for ministry. If your church has more than one pastor on staff, then do the exercise separately with each pastor. Talk openly about differences in priorities, and seek to understand the reasons for which members of the group and the pastor may differ on the importance assigned to a particular item.

What's Most Important?

Make copies of this page for the pastor and for each member of the executive committee, pastor parish committee, church board, or other group responsible for supervising and supporting the pastor. Have each person work individually to rank the importance of each item on the list in the pastor's work–using the symbols provided below. Share results and talk candidly with one another.

VI = **Very Important for the pastor to do**
I = **Important but not the highest priority**
NP = **Necessary but not a priority**
O = **Optional depending on time available**
SE = **Someone Else should do this instead of the pastor**

___ 1. Sermon and worship preparation and leadership.
___ 2. Teaching Sunday school.
___ 3. Helping equip Sunday school teachers.
___ 4. Giving guidance to the stewardship campaign.
___ 5. Leading the stewardship campaign.
___ 6. Developing the devotional life to be a spiritual leader.
___ 7. Visiting people who are in the hospital.
___ 8. Conducting funerals.
___ 9. Helping those who are living with grief and loss.
___10. Conducting weddings for members.
___11. Conducting weddings for nonmembers.
___12. Doing premarital counseling.
___13. Unlocking the church for meetings.
___14. Supervising the maintenance of the church property.
___15. Studying to stay current on church management, theology, etc.
___16. Spending occasional time with the youth group.
___17. Being an advisor for the youth group.
___18. Handling correspondence.
___19. Advising the church board and other church groups.
___20. Staying on top of the mission of the church.
___21. Being a leader who makes things happen in the church.
___22. Being an enabler who helps others make things happen.
___23. Helping members develop their spiritual gifts.
___24. Helping the church develop a clear vision for its future.
___25. Training people to reach the unchurched.
___26. Taking time away from the church for continuing education and spiritual renewal.
___27. Working cooperatively with other pastors and churches in the community or areas of mutual concern.
___28. Working cooperatively with denominational agencies to strengthen the denomination as a whole.

Church leadership should not attempt to control all that the pastor does with his or her time. There certainly are minimal obligations which clergy should meet, and some authorities refer to those as "paying the rent." Those obligations should be clearly understood by the pastor and the church. But clergy also need discretionary time and the ability to set many of their own priorities. If the church wants the pastor to show true leadership, it's crucial to extend the latitude which makes that possible. Discretionary work time permits pastors to build the relationships and plan the strategies which make positive change possible. Time that the pastor spends in prayer, Bible study, reading, and continuing education can often result in new vision and inspiration which motivate both the minister and the congregation to do great things in the name of Christ.

2. Be sure your pastor is taking sufficient time for his or her family and protecting time for vacations and continuing education. Talk with the pastor about this concern. If your pastor is married, find out how his or her spouse feels about the demands on the pastor's time.

Vacations are sometimes a problem for pastors who are not earning large salaries. This constitutes a justice issue, and churches whose pastors can't afford vacations need to examine the salary being paid. It's also important for the pastor to have time for continuing education opportunities. Be alert for ways in which the church may be able to encourage the pastor to have more family time, participate in continuing education, and have good vacations. For example:

- Church members can volunteer to provide child care so the pastor and his or her spouse can have time together.

- A church family with a condominium on the beach or a cabin in the woods can offer the use of the facility without charge for the pastor and family.

- A special church offering can be taken to provide a vacation or continuing education opportunity for the pastor. This isn't a substitute for an adequate salary for the pastor and for continuing education money in the church budget, but a special effort every three or four years may be appreciated. Many pastors, for example, are renewed by a trip to the Holy Land.

- Encourage your pastor to take a sabbatical at whatever the recommended frequency is in your denomination.

Few pastors feel comfortable bringing up the topic of a sabbatical on their own, but most pastors can benefit significantly from an extended change of pace. The time that the pastor is gone can also be an opportunity for further development of lay leadership within the church.

The group in the church which supervises and supports the pastor should help arrange pastoral care and pulpit supply during those times that the minister is on vacation or away at a continuing education event. Churches which are served by more than one pastor can handle this situation through the careful scheduling of vacations and continuing education. Those with a single pastor need to make arrangements for a lay person, a retired pastor, or the pastor of a neighboring congregation to provide pastoral care and pulpit supply. The costs of that coverage need to come from the church rather than from the pastor.

There should also be a clear understanding about what should be done if a church member dies while the pastor is gone. Many churches do not expect the pastor to interrupt his or her vacation or continuing education time to return for a funeral. The funeral is handled by the person or persons who are providing pastoral care. Some churches and some pastors, however, are not comfortable with this approach. If there is consensus that the pastor should return for the funeral of a church member, then the church needs to be prepared to pay for the cost of that return and to provide additional time away to compensate for what was lost.

3. Pastors need honest feedback. Problems should be discussed directly with the pastor rather than talked about behind his or her back. Don't wait for the annual staff evaluation meeting or even for a regular meeting of your board or committee. If there is a problem which the pastor should know about, go directly to him or her to discuss it. Few things are more frustrating to a clergy person than the discovery that many people in the church are talking about an issue of which he or she wasn't even aware. For example:

- A church family was greatly distressed that the pastor did not make a visit following the death of an out-of-town relative. The pastor did not know about the death or about the family's unhappiness for weeks.

- A pastor who felt it was important to be sure that several elements were present in each service of worship often let Sunday morning services go over the expected quitting time by ten to twenty minutes. Only a few people ever said anything to the pastor about this, and those persons always did so in a half-joking way, as though it was not really important. In truth, a large number of people were very frustrated with the pastor for what they took to be a lack of respect for their time.

- A former pastor had always taken the initiative in scheduling infant dedications with new parents. A new pastor had been in a previous parish where others told her when they wanted to schedule a dedication. She felt that it would be pushy to suggest people have a dedication on a particular Sunday. Three households were upset about not being approached by the pastor, but the pastor went months without knowing this expectation existed.

Speaking directly with the pastor about problems should not, however, become an excuse for routinely attacking the pastor's self-esteem or for presenting little issues as though they were major concerns. Remember Steve Clapp's **Four for One Rule:**

> *You should have shared appreciation for at least four things before you share a criticism or suggestion for change.*

That's a good rule not only for relationships with pastors but also with other volunteers in the church and other people in one's life. Sharing positive feedback creates an openness to suggestions for change when needed. Don't limit feedback to the pastor to those times when problems arise. Share appreciation on a regular basis.

In his book *Negative Criticism*, Sidney Simon suggests six filters we should use before expressing our disappointment with someone [pp. 67-73]:

- *Is the person in any shape to receive this criticism right now? . . .*
- *Are you willing to stay around long enough to help pick up the pieces? . . .*
- *How many times has the person heard this criticism before? . . .*
- *Can the person do anything about it? . . .*
- *Are you positive that none of your own hang-ups, your own deep-seated psychological needs, hurts or fears, are*

causing you to make this criticism? . . .
- Are you sure that what this person needs is another criticism; wouldn't they be better off or better motivated to change by some appreciation or validation instead? . . .

But if the criticism is going to be offered, *always* share it directly with the pastor.

4. Interpret the work of the pastor and other staff to the congregation. Help people understand why time off is important and why a new pastor may do something differently than the last pastor. Clear and frequent communication is very helpful and quickly deals with murmurings within the congregation. Here are some strategies:

- Some of the very best communication happens on a one-to-one basis. If each member of the board or committee takes the initiative to speak with persons in the congregation about the pastor's work, positive word-of-mouth will make a great difference. For example:

    - "Our pastor is working hard to blend some more contemporary elements into our worship services. She feels that if this doesn't happen, we will start to lose some of our younger members and won't be able to attract new people. We need for people to understand why the music is changing."

    - "We were very concerned to learn in executive committee that our pastor has been working eighty hours a week all winter. That feels like too much to us, and we're urging the pastor to start taking more time off."

    - "Some members have been critical because the new pastor hasn't been sitting with people the entire time that a family member is in surgery. He feels that he can be most effective for the church as a whole by coming in time to say a prayer before surgery and to check on the patient and the family a day or so after the surgery. Our committee has looked at the pastor's work load and agrees with him. We're training some lay volunteers to sit with families who would like that kind of presence while waiting."

- There are also times when concerns like those shared above and other matters need to be addressed to the whole congregation during announcements or a joys and concerns time.

- The church newsletter can be a helpful means of communication about issues involving the pastor's work.

- Churches with a tradition of congregational meetings can use those as opportunities to share information which the church should know about the pastor and his or her work.

5. Encourage your pastor through notes, phone calls, and unexpected gifts. When the pastor has an especially excellent sermon, write a note saying so–or pick up the phone and call. When the pastor has done a good job handling a controversial issue in a board meeting, share your appreciation. Here are some other suggestions:

- Give the pastor a gift certificate from a local restaurant as an expression of your appreciation.

- Designate a week as "Pastor Appreciation Week," and make plans to involve the congregation. Have people write notes, send flowers, provide dinner, and in other ways convey their appreciation.

- If your congregation provides "notes of encouragement" which can be sent to persons going through difficult times, remind them that the pastor may also appreciate such notes!

- Invite the pastor and family to be your guests for an evening out–or take care of the children so the pastor and spouse can have an evening by themselves.

- Have each member bring one carnation on a Sunday morning and make a bouquet for the pastor.

Think about what would be meaningful to you if you were the pastor or a member of the pastor's family!

6. Be an advocate for the pastor in dealing with overly critical or antagonistic members. Minor criticisms of the pastor and misunderstandings about the pastor's work occur in even the healthiest congregations served by the healthiest clergy. Some congregations, however, are plagued by a small number of persons–often only one or two–who are frankly antagonistic toward the pastor and sometimes toward others in church leadership. Such persons are often very active in the church and function in a dependency mode. These persons may also believe that they are more spiritual than the pastor or the rest of the congregation. Because they either work covertly, in passive aggressive ways, or express their opinions very forcefully, church members often avoid sharing differing points of view.

The pastor, and sometimes the pastor's family as well, can be very vulnerable to the attacks of such persons. If the pastor defends himself or herself forcefully, it can appear as an attack on the member. The group in the church responsible for the supervision and support of the pastor has a responsibility to help the pastor deal with such situations. It may be necessary for one or two members of that group to have a caring confrontation with the antagonistic member. There can also be times when an outside consultant or mediator is appropriate.

The group needs to be a safe place for the pastor to share his or her concerns on such issues, and it needs to function in a supportive way. One or two antagonistic members can severely undermine the effectiveness of the pastor's ministry, and members who are permitted to function in that way ultimately harm themselves as well.

7. Work with pastoral leadership to develop expectations and policies for other church staff members. Space in this relatively brief booklet doesn't permit a full overview of the work of nonpastoral staff, but it's important to recognize that their effectiveness will often have direct impact on pastoral effectiveness. Many of the observations about clergy shared in these pages also apply to other professional staff such as Christian education directors, youth workers, music directors, organists, parish visitors, parish nurses, and business administrators.

It's important not to undervalue the contribution of support staff such as secretaries and custodians. The church should be clear about expectations and fair in compensation and benefits with those persons. Administrative and financial secretaries often have confidential information about church members, and there need to be clear policies about the handling of that information. Violations of that confidentiality can have a negative impact on the pastor's work and on the congregation.

8. Pray for the pastor and other staff! The power that can be unleashed through concerted prayer for your pastor and staff will simply amaze you! And it will bring honor and glory to God! Make prayer for your pastor a regular part of your prayer life. When you are aware of special challenges or difficulties facing the pastor or the church, pray about those matters.

If you are seeking to deepen your own prayer life, you can find guidance in many resources including: *Too Busy Not to Pray* by Bill Hybels; *Prayer* by Richard Foster; *Letters to Malcolm–Chiefly on Prayer* by C.S. Lewis; and *Reflections on Prayer* by Thomas Merton.

9. Be realistic in expectations of the pastor's spouse and children. Congregations too often have unrealistic expectations of the pastor's spouse and children. It's important to remember that, with the exception of husband-wife co-pastorates, the spouse and children are not part of the employment agreement! It's never fair to expect the pastor's spouse to accept particular responsibilities in the church. The spouse is not an unpaid assistant to the pastor, is not an automatic Sunday school teacher, and is not required to be a member of a fellowship organization. Obviously the congregation is delighted when the pastor's spouse wants to be heavily involved in the life of the church, but that needs to be by choice rather than expectation. The group which supervises and supports the pastor needs to be a positive advocate for the pastor's family–protecting them against unfair expectations and reaching out to them.

Many of us have heard the pastor's children referred to as PKs (Preacher's Kids) and not always with fondness. Life can be difficult for the children of clergy. Almost any behavior can be called into question, as though different standards apply to the pastor's children than to others in the congregation. Noise that we accept from other children may not be tolerated from the pastor's family. A pastor's son with long hair and a tattoo can receive criticism that would not be directed to another young person in the congregation.

Some people maintain that the pastor and his or her family should not form close friendships within the congregation because that can make them appear to be too strongly influenced by particular people. This can be an unrealistic expectation, especially because the pastor's schedule often makes it difficult to have significant relationships outside the congregation. It is not possible for the pastor and family to be "best friends" with everyone in the church! We should not deny them the opportunity of having a few especially close relationships within the church, and we should not be offended when those relationships are not with us!

Show the pastor's family the same kind of appreciation, acceptance, understanding, and love you would want if you were in the same situation. Follow your heart and the Spirit within you to share Christ's love with them.

10. Be fair, honest, open, and kind in all negotiations with the pastor. While there are exceptions, the majority of pastors find it uncomfortable to assertively represent themselves in negotiations on salary, retirement, expenses, vacation, and related matters. Those serving on the group responsible for the supervision and support of the pastor need to take the initiative in seeing that negotiations and discussions on these matters are responsibly and fairly handled. Here are some questions to consider:

- Do you have a set time each year when salary and other matters are discussed? Does the pastor always know in advance when these conversations will take place? Is the pastor encouraged to be part of these conversations and to express his or her needs and concerns?

- Does the committee or board responsible seek information about what other churches provide for their pastors? That information is usually available from denominational executives, and it's also possible to call other congregations of comparable size in the area. Does the committee or board consider what other congregations do or what the denomination recommends as the upper limit, or does it proactively seek to reward and help the pastor in as many ways as possible?

- Does the salary fairly reflect the cost of living, the level of pay other professionals in the community receive, the importance of the pastor to the congregation, and the expectations of the pastor? If you were the pastor, would you feel good about the pay you receive?

- If a parsonage is provided, is it in good condition? What improvements would make it a more pleasant home? If a housing allowance is provided, is it fair, and does it provide an adequate home for the pastor and his or her family?

- Are good health insurance benefits provided? Does the insurance encourage preventive health exams from family physicians, dentists, and ophthalmologists? Some denominational health insurance plans are more expensive for younger clergy than privately obtained insurance, but the reason is often because that plan is providing for older and retired clergy. There may be a good case for participating in the denominational plan, even if it is not the cheapest available, providing it offers good benefits. Consider the possibility of an allowance to the pastor to pay for insurance deductibles, eye care, and dental care.

- Are adequate retirement benefits provided for the pastor? This may include participation in the denominational pension fund, an IRA, a housing equity fund (to let those who live in parsonages accumulate some money toward the purchase of a house at retirement), and other retirement benefits.

- Does the budget provide adequate expense reimbursement for the pastor? Is the mileage rate for reimbursement at least equal to what the IRS permits? Has any consideration been given to leasing a car for the pastor, which can have tax benefits for the pastor in some circumstances? Is the pastor reimbursed for hospitality expenses such as purchasing lunch for members, entertaining in the home, and giving small gifts to leaders?

- Does the budget provide for the continued growth and development of the pastor? Are there funds for continuing education? Is there a "book and journal" budget item which encourages the pastor to read the latest resources available? Can the pastor attend a seminar or workshop without spending his or her own money? Is there any budgetary provision for the expenses of a sabbatical every few years?

- Are expectations of the pastor about the number of hours worked and the priorities for ministry clear? Are any differences between the board or committee and the pastor talked through until there is mutual agreement? Does the committee or board respect the pastor as a professional?

The Congregation–
Supporting and Encouraging The Pastor

1. Seek to better understand the pastor's work. There are similarities between the pastor's work and that of some other professionals (such as teachers, principals, physicians, social workers, and counselors). But no other professional relates to as large a group of people as a congregation in the same way that a pastor does. This doesn't mean that the pastor's work is more important or difficult than that of people in the congregation–all of us as Christians are called to be disciples, to follow Christ in all that we do. You can, however, better enable the pastor's work by understanding the unique nature of his or her vocation. Here are some further observations about the pastor's work:

- The pastor works with people through crises, including severe illness, death, and grief. While medical professionals and funeral home directors relate to people during difficult times, their relationships do not continue long-term in the same way as the pastor, who will see the individual or family members week after week.

- In the same week or even the same day, the pastor may spend time with a person who is dying, celebrate the birth of a child, and talk with a couple who are planning to get married. Living with both the highs and the lows of people in the congregation is a part of daily life for the pastor.

- The pastor may be counseling a couple whose marriage is in trouble but also continuing to work with those persons in the life of the church. The pastor must keep the problem as a confidence and relate positively to the couple in all settings. This is not the same as a professional counselor who sees the couple once a week for an hour and focuses only on their marriage problems.

- The pastor is expected to have a reasonably high level of professional skills in rather diverse areas. He or she is generally the most knowledgeable person in the church about the Bible, church history, theology, and ethics. The pastor is expected to have counseling skills, administrative skills, and outstanding communication skills. The pastor also needs to have knowledge in areas such as Christian education, youth work, evangelism, worship, and stewardship. Most people look to the pastor as an expert on prayer and the spiritual life. But no person can be equally strong in all these areas.

- Because of the pastor's unique involvement in the lives of people through both the highs and lows which come, people form bonds with the pastor that are especially strong and have expectations of the pastor for intimacy and availability which they are less likely to have of a physician or a professional counselor. As a result, people have a tendency to want close friendships with the pastor and the pastor's family. If the pastor and his or her family are invited into a home for dinner, is that part of the pastor's work or the pastor's free time? Is the pastor truly free to accept or reject such invitations without damaging relationships with people?

- No matter how skilled in organization the pastor may be, crises in the lives of church members can completely change the most carefully made plans. If there are several hospitalizations and two deaths in the same week, the pastor may have difficulty accomplishing any routine work. People may not always understand the complexity of factors which make the pastor unavailable when they want to speak with him or her about non-crisis matters.

- The pastor must often be the mediator between strongly divergent feelings in the church. Tensions often emerge, for example, over the style of worship services. Long-time church members are more likely to want services to be relatively traditional and to include organ music and well known hymns. Newer members and visitors may want to see greater diversity in worship with more use of drama, video, and contemporary music. The pastor often feels caught in the middle between those views.

- The pastor must also deal with sometimes conflicting expectations of his or her work. There are those in the congregation who expect the pastor to exert significant leadership and help the church move in new directions. There are others who resent the pastor showing too much leadership and who expect the pastor to work as an employee, doing what he or she is told.

- And the pastor, in all of his or her work, is seeking to respond to God's call and direction. While the pastor may be matched to the congregation by a denominational structure and may have an employment contract with the church, the pastor's ultimate professional accountability is to God rather than to any human organization. All of us, of course, are accountable to God for the manner in which we live; but the pastor generally experiences this reality in a somewhat different way.

How can you learn more about the pastor's work? We hope reading this booklet will be one helpful strategy–not only this chapter but also the chapters which are addressed to the pastor and to the group responsible for supervising and supporting the pastor. You can also learn by listening, observing, and asking questions. You can interact not only with the pastor but also with the committee or board which supervises and supports the pastor.

2. Think about the expectations which you and others have of the pastor. Are your expectations fair? Church members in some traditions expect that the pastor will sit with the family when a family member has surgery. But that may be unrealistic when several people are ill at the same time, or when the congregation is large, or when there are many other expectations on the pastor. Members should be open to receiving help from other persons who have been trained for that purpose.

Some small congregations have come to expect that the pastor will take care of opening the church on Sunday morning, turning on the lights, and turning up the heat. If the pastor lives in a parsonage beside the church, he or she is the person who is closest and can most readily do so. But Sunday morning brings for the pastor the responsibility for leading worship,

Strengthening Pastoral Ministry

sometimes the responsibility for teaching a class, and always the need to be available and open to people who come. The church may benefit by making it possible for the pastor to have time for prayer and a review of the sermon, while someone else unlocks the church.

Are there other areas in which the pastor is expected to do things which others in the church could readily do? If you identify such areas, talk with the pastor about them. You may be able to become the pastor's advocate in working to change those expectations.

A pastor in a busy, growing church began to realize that he had almost no Friday or Saturday evenings which were free in the spring or summer. The church had a large number of weddings, and the weddings were generally held on Saturday evening or Sunday afternoon with the rehearsal the previous night. The pastor, of course, needed to conduct the rehearsal as well as the wedding, and it had become expected that both he and his wife would attend the lengthy rehearsal dinners and wedding receptions. He felt very close to almost all the persons for whom he performed marriage services, but the time demands were making it very difficult to be with his family. The pastor began scheduling rehearsals at slightly earlier times and stopped going to rehearsal dinners and wedding receptions. That gained him valuable time with his family. People initially felt hurt by this decision; but those who reflected on it carefully realized that the pastor needed the family time more than the church family needed his presence at rehearsal dinners and receptions.

Increasing numbers of small churches are served by bivocational pastors. These pastors generally work many hours a week at secular employment and also give ministerial leadership to the church. Because the church is not their only source of income, they can offer pastoral care to congregations which could not afford a full-time minister. Some of them find significant opportunities to witness to their faith in their secular work, and that employment may give them insights into what congregational members experience in their own jobs. It's important to have fair expectations of bivocational pastors, who will generally have more limitations on their time and availability than a full-time minister.

3. Assess your own ability to accept change. If you want your church to grow and become healthier, that means change will happen. And the pastor probably will have to change his or her priorities to facilitate those changes in the church. Most of us like to think of ourselves as being open to change, but we are sometimes not as open as we think!

Many congregations adopt mission or vision statements which call for growth and outreach but fail to fully recognize the implications for the pastor. In congregational surveys conducted by Christian Community, over 90% of the members of almost all churches agree that reaching new people is important. Yet when asked if outreach to the unchurched should be as important in the pastor's use of time as ministry to those who are members, only 34% in the typical congregation agree. The reality is that few churches can grow without significant leadership from the pastor, and that means the pastor must find time to spend on growth and outreach concerns.

Congregations, like all organizations of people, are complex systems. Sometimes the systems are healthy, and sometimes they are unhealthy. When we are in the midst of congregational life, it is not always easy for us to recognize how much the systems affect what we do and how we respond to changes which occur. Every congregation is comprised of a unique mix of believers, each with a different personality. At our very best, we are a wonderful blend, working together to share the good news of Jesus Christ. At our worst, we drive others away from the church. Chuck Swindoll, in *Strengthening Your Grip*, compares this unhealthy behavior to that of porcupines on a frigid winter night [p. 32]:

> *The cold drives us closer together into a tight huddle to keep warm. As we begin to snuggle really close, our sharp quills cause us to jab and prick each other- a condition which forces us apart. But before long we start getting cold, so we move back to get warm again, only to stab and puncture each other once more. And so we participate in this strange, rhythmic "Tribal dance." We cannot deny it, we need each other, yet we needle each other.*

Consider this situation. A medium-sized congregation has a Sunday school class of middle-aged people who see themselves being responsible for the welfare of the church. The members of that class occupy most of the key leadership positions in the congregation. Many of them are concerned that newer members of the church, who are in their young adult years, travel frequently on weekends and are not as regular in attendance as long-time church members.

Strengthening Pastoral Ministry

The pastor knew in her heart and in her mind that putting young adults in leadership was the best way to increase their commitment to the church and to help the church be more open to change. There were no young adults on the church board or most of the committees, so she began encouraging changes in the composition of those groups.

Members of the middle-aged Sunday school class became greatly concerned about the proposed changes in leadership and began talking about that issue rather than about the curriculum topic. Several members approached the pastor and urged that inexperienced people not be put in positions of leadership. Because of their pressure, the pastor backed off her plans to involve more young adults.

Young adults, in general, are not enthused about committee meetings; but the pastor had convinced some of the importance of that kind of involvement. She regretted telling those she had convinced to serve that they were not needed. The result, as she had sadly anticipated, was that several young adults felt they had no say in the decisions of the church and left. Members of the middle-aged class were not upset, feeling that the young adults who had been coming weren't really the "right kind" for the church.

The class of course didn't dislike young adults, and they didn't see themselves being a power group in the church. The reality, however, was that they feared the changes which would come with young adults participating more fully in decisions. They would also have suffered a loss of identity if not filling so many key positions in the life of the church.

One of our greatest testimonies to the world is for those outside the church to "see how much we love each other." It was that love that attracted others to the first Christians, and it is that same love that will bring others to our churches. So let's make the most of our blend of strengths and weaknesses for the sake of the kingdom! And that includes learning to be genuinely open to change!

4. Seek opportunities to share appreciation and encouragement with the pastor. Here are some easy and practical things you can do:

- When the pastor shares a sermon that touches your life in a significant way, write a note of appreciation. While kind words on the way out of church are appreciated, a note can be read more than once. Most pastors cherish that kind of encouragement.

- When you know the pastor is experiencing conflicting expectations over the style of worship or another matter, take the time to tell the pastor that you appreciate the efforts he or she is making to help the church, even if you don't agree with all the changes being made.

- Give the pastor and his or her family a gift certificate to a restaurant. Bookstore gift certificates are also great gifts for pastors, almost all of whom love to read.

The previous chapter shares some suggestions for members of the committee or board responsible for supervising and supporting the pastor. The encouragement strategies shared there can be practiced by almost anyone in the congregation.

5. If you have a significant criticism or concern about the pastor's work, share it directly with the pastor. Think carefully about the validity of the concern before sharing it. If it is simply a matter of personal preference or a very small matter, it may be best to say nothing. Note the discussion on sharing criticism in the previous chapter. But if it is a criticism which is important for the pastor to hear or if you can't help sharing the concern with other people, then you need to take it directly to the minister. When the criticisms and concerns do not go directly to the pastor, several things can happen:

- When the pastor learns about the criticism at a later time and realizes that it has been a topic of conversation in the church, it is almost impossible for he or she not to feel defensive. This increases the probability of conflict and makes discussion more difficult. When spoken to directly and in a supportive way, it is much easier for the pastor to be open and to genuinely hear the concern.

- Change is not likely to happen if the pastor is not informed of the problem. Out of frustration, people in the church who are unhappy sometimes seek to build support for their position outside the formal decision-making channels of the church. This has the potential to produce division in the church.

- If the concerns are serious but not ones on which people agree, then sides can start to be drawn–all the time without the pastor being aware there is a serious problem. If the pastor has opportunity to address issues at an early stage, congregational conflict can often be avoided.

- By not hearing the reasons for which the pastor has acted in a particular way, it can be easy for a concern to be blown out of proportion to its importance. When you speak directly to the pastor, you often discover reasons for a particular action which cause you to feel differently.

6. Seek to view issues and concerns in the church from a Christian perspective rather than from the consumer perspective of secular society. We live in a fast-paced culture in which we increasingly pick-and-choose from a plethora of options in products and services. When we become dissatisfied with a restaurant or store, we simply change to a different one. We evaluate products and services from the perspective of our own needs and desires rather than from the perspective of the larger community. When we have conflicts, our inclination is to develop a strategy for protecting our own interests or reaching a middle-ground rather than seeking the just and equitable resolution for all affected by the conflict.

In the church, we are challenged to live out of different standards, following the teachings of Christ. For example:

- Christ encourages us to care not only about the meeting of our own needs but also about the needs of others. Rather than being critical of worship elements which do not meet our personal preferences, we need to consider the value that those elements may have to other persons in the congregation.

- When conflicts arise concerning the pastor or others in the church, our faith should challenge us to seek resolutions which are just and equitable for everyone.

- When discussing difficult issues or communicating negative feedback, we should do so with kindness and genuine concern for the person with whom we are talking. We should also be open to the possibility that we could be the ones at fault.

- As a member of the church, we belong not just to a human institution but to the body of Christ. The love of Christ brings us together with persons who may have different backgrounds, opinions, and preferences than our own. That is part of the strength of the church at its best. We need to celebrate differences rather than being threatened by them. And we need to recognize that the pastor is called to minister not only to us but to the entire congregation.

7. Practice spiritual disciplines personally and corporately including prayers for the pastor and the pastor's family. Developing our own spiritual lives helps make us healthier members of the church and enriches all that we do. Seek opportunities through Sunday school classes and small groups to deepen the spiritual life, Develop a personal time of prayer and devotional reflection each day, perhaps using a publication like *The Upper Room* as a guide. Note the books on prayer which are recommended on page 35.

During your prayers, include the needs of the church and of the pastor. Pray for the health and well-being of the pastor's family. Pray for openness to change in your own life and in the life of the church.

8. Learn to recognize your own spiritual gifts and the ministries to which you are called. Protestant and Anabaptist traditions affirm not only the concept of the priesthood of all believers but also the belief that God has given us gifts to be used in service to the church and to others. Some people think of spiritual gifts narrowly like speaking in tongues or having the gift of healing, but most spiritual gifts are not spectacular or controversial.

While we identify the ministry of the church with professional clergy, the reality is that ministry is the task of each one of us. God has given all of us gifts to be used in Christ's service. Read carefully the comments about spiritual gifts which appear on page 22 of this booklet. The publication *Preaching, Planning, and Plumbing*, listed at the end of this booklet, can be a valuable resource in identifying your spiritual gifts.

Knowing your own spiritual gifts can of course help you be aware of areas in which you can be of special help to your pastor and to your church as an institution. The more important reason for being aware of gifts, however, is that those gifts should help focus your personal ministry in the most effective ways.

Strengthening Pastoral Ministry

Most of us have between two and five spiritual gifts, and we should seek to maximize those gifts in our ministries and in our lives. That doesn't mean, of course, that we only work within the areas of our spiritual gifts. Every local church has numerous important tasks that must be done, whether someone feels gifted in each of those areas or not! To the extent that it is possible, however, people are more fulfilled and energized when they work in their areas of giftedness. That reality is true of laypersons in the church as well as clergy. It's also true for those working in secular settings. Discovering the strengths for your own ministry can enable you to further the ministry of your congregation and of your pastor. We are all in ministry together, by the grace of God.

When Change Comes

No pastor serves the same congregation forever. Each year tens of thousands of churches across the country go through the transition from one minister to another. These changes happen for a wide variety of reasons:

- The pastor feels called to ministry at a different location which offers new opportunities and challenges.
- The church feels that the pastor does not meet the needs of the congregation and that a change should come.
- The pastor feels that he or she can no longer function effectively in the congregation and that a change is needed.
- The denominational structure determines that the pastor is needed in a different ministry setting.
- The church faces financial problems which make it impossible to continue the level of compensation which the pastor needs.
- The church develops new priorities for ministry which necessitate staff changes.
- The pastor experiences health problems which make it impossible to continue.
- The pastor dies.
- The pastor retires.
- The pastor decides to leave the ministry.
- A bivocational pastor feels the need to concentrate again on the secular job, for which he or she also feels a true calling.
- A bivocational or other part-time minister decides to move into a full-time ministry position.
- A minister in the free or plural ministry tradition decides to leave pastoral leadership and extend the opportunity to others.

The reasons for the change obviously have significant impact on the church, the departing pastor, and the new pastor. When a pastor chooses to retire at the end of a long and fruitful ministry in a congregation, there usually is considerable notice to help the church in its planning for transition; and both the church and the retiring pastor can celebrate what has been accomplished. When the church has determined that the pastor no longer can function effectively in that setting, the process can be very painful for everyone–particularly if the pastor does not share that view.

A booklet of this length cannot give a comprehensive treatment of the issues and concerns involved in pastoral transitions. In this short chapter, we offer a few perspectives which may be helpful to the minister and the congregation.

1. Church leaders need to be realistic in thinking about the pastor and his or her work. It's easy to fall into the trap of putting the entire responsibility for the health of the church on the shoulders of the pastor. If a congregation has been in decline through the last three pastors, then the reasons for the decline are not necessarily in the quality of pastoral leadership. The problems may be in the hospitality and the attitude of the congregation or in the limited potential in the geographical area served by the church. The church may need a transition in congregational attitudes rather than a transition in pastoral leadership. Use of instruments like the LifeQuest Congregational Survey (available from New Life Ministries) can be helpful in determining what dynamics exist within the congregation.

2. Pastors need to be open and honest with church leaders in talking about their desire for a change. In many denominations, advancement comes by moving to a larger parish or to a position with significant administrative responsibility. Pastors who have proven very effective may come to feel that it is time to advance and truly feel a call to another situation. When that happens, they need to be open with church leaders and at the right time with the congregation as a whole. They should not make it appear that the denomination has "forced" them to move to a larger church against their will–that destroys confidence in the system by which pastors are matched with churches.

A pastor can also feel called to a new position for reasons that have little to do with professional advancement. There may be a feeling that he or she has accomplished what is possible in the present location or a desire to accept a new challenge. There may also be a deep-seated frustration with the inability to bring about change in the current position. Again, openness from the pastor brings about healthy dialogue and helps the church in the decisions it makes. If the pastor wants to move because the current situation feels too frustrating or unhealthy, the church needs to hear that concern.

3. **Church leaders need to be open and honest with pastors in talking about their desire for a change.** As shared repeatedly in this booklet, church leaders and members need to be open with the pastor about their concerns on a continuing basis. If church leaders no longer have confidence in the pastor's ability or feel that a pastor with a different style would be of significant help, then they need to say so with as much kindness as possible. The desire to avoid confrontation sometimes causes church leaders to give favorable evaluations to pastors when they are actually not satisfied. The dissatisfaction builds over time and may eventually escalate to a destructive explosion. More honest communication along the way offers the possibility of the pastor and the church changing in positive ways. If needed change does not come, then the desire for a new pastor will not be a surprise.

4. **Pastors and churches need to recognize that there are times when the match between them is simply not right.** The process of matching the right pastor to the right church is a very complicated one, regardless of denominational tradition. It is difficult in denominations which centralize the authority for pastoral changes in a bishop or other administrative person, and it is difficult in denominations which permit the congregation to hire and fire the pastor. Sometimes, in spite of the best efforts and intentions of everyone involved, the match is simply not right. The gifts which the pastor has are not the ones which the church most needs, or there are differences of style or approach which cannot be resolved. When such situations occur, both the pastor and the church benefit by being honest with each other about the need for a change without blaming one another.

5. **Clergy and churches need to recognize that pastors have a variety of spiritual gifts and also a variety of styles of ministry.** Differences in spiritual gifts have been discussed earlier in this booklet. Pastors can also differ considerably in their primary styles or approaches to ministry. Those differences grow out of personality, education, experience, and assessment of the needs of the church. There are pastors who:

- Clearly take the initiative as leaders, casting a vision and directing the church into the future.

- Are very process oriented and work more slowly with the congregation, helping them develop a vision.
- Focus heavily on the administration of the church and see themselves primarily implementing the decisions of others.
- See themselves primarily as spiritual leaders, placing emphasis on preaching and teaching rather than on program or administration.
- Place their greatest priority on the pastoral care of the congregation.

There are a variety of systems available for categorizing pastors by style and churches by type. One such system, *Personality Type and Religious Leadership* by Roy M. Oswald and Otto Kroeger, looks at ministerial style as revealed by the "Myers-Briggs Type Indicator" (MBTI).

What style does your church need? If your church has been in decline, you may well need a pastor who will show strong proactive leadership and take the initiative. That may be difficult if the congregation is accustomed to a more process-oriented pastor or one who focuses primarily on pastoral care. When going through a pastoral transition, it's important to reflect on the nature of the congregation and to identify the characteristics of a new minister which are most important.

6. Many congregations benefit from having an interim pastor before a new pastor comes. Interim pastors are sometimes inevitable because of the length of time required to find a new pastor, but there are other valuable reasons to consider an interim. For example:

- If the pastor who is leaving has been deeply loved and has been serving the church for ten years or longer, an interim may help the congregation deal with the grief of losing that pastor and prepare to welcome a new pastor.
- If the church has experienced significant conflict with the pastor who is leaving, then an interim can provide time for healing and self-examination by the church.
- If the church recognizes that it is in transition and needs time and study to determine the best style of pastor to call, an interim can give leadership through that time and often help with the study process.

Most denominations are increasingly recognizing the importance of interim pastorates, and some have pastors who specialize in interim situations. The best interim pastor for your church will generally be one who has done interims before or who has received some training in dealing with the issues an interim is likely to confront. While the decision about an interim will generally be made much more quickly than the decision about a new pastor, it is still a very important decision.

7. Church leaders and the congregation need to seek the warmest ways possible to say farewell to one pastor and welcome to another. Churches should think about questions like these:

- How can the church best encourage prayer for the pastors and for the life of the congregation?
- What kind of celebration of a pastor's service will be most meaningful?
- What would the departing pastor's family appreciate?
- How can people in the congregation be given opportunity to express their appreciation for the pastor's service?
- What assistance would the pastor appreciate in the process of moving out of a church office and parsonage?
- What needs to be done to the church office and the parsonage to welcome the new pastor?
- What kinds of orientation will the new pastor need?
- What can be done to help the spouse and children of the new pastor feel welcome?
- What kinds of events will help the new pastor get acquainted with the congregation?
- How can the church best facilitate the moving process?

8. Pastors who are in transition should seek to function in the most helpful way possible to the congregation. Pastors who are leaving a congregation need to remember that the way they leave will be remembered! Acts of kindness, affirmation, and encouragement to the church can make things easier for the arrival of the next pastor. Endeavor to leave records and resources which will help the new pastor in his or her work. If you know who will be following you, resist the temptation to say critical things about that person.

New pastors have a wonderful opportunity before them for a fresh start! Be careful not to speak critically of the work of the pastor being replaced. Take time to get acquainted with the congregation, and be prepared to move ahead with new initiatives when the timing is right. Cultivate your devotional life and others habits that lead to healthy ministry.

Strengthening Pastoral Ministry

Discussion Questions

The discussion questions which follow are primarily designed for congregational groups which are studying this booklet. They may also be helpful for pastors, church leaders, and individual members who are reflecting privately on the booklet. Consider opening and closing sessions with prayer.

Session One: *Introduction and The Tension* [pages 5-12]
1. Read **Philippians 2:1-5**. Note especially these words: "Do nothing from selfish ambition or conceit; but in humility regard others as better than yourselves." What do those words suggest for pastors? For congregations? Why is it difficult to follow those words in contemporary North American society? What other biblical passages seem to you important for pastors and churches?
2. Were you surprised by the percentages of clergy reported on pages 5 and 6 who indicate being harmed in various ways by the ministry? Why, or why not? Can a pastor stay healthy in a congregation that is not? Why, or why not?
3. Why is it easy for pastors to get caught in a performance-based approach to ministry [see pages 8-10]? Why is it important for pastors to be concerned about their effectiveness? How can an overemphasis on performance lead to burnout?
4. Note the quote on page 10 from *Change and the Established Congregation*. Are there two separate congregations in your church? What other pressures are put on our churches by rapid changes in society?
5. Pages 10-12 contain examples of healthy pastors making a difference in congregations. What are your experiences about the impact that a healthy, effective pastor can have?

Session Two: *Taking Care of Yourself-A Guide for Pastors* [pages 13-25]
1. The checklist on physical fitness on pages 14-15 applies to all people, not just pastors. Complete the checklist and talk about it with others. Ask your pastor, if he or she is willing, to share responses to the checklist.
2. Eleven areas for self-care and organization by pastors are identified in this chapter. Which ones would be the greatest

challenges to you personally? Which ones do you think are most difficult for a pastor? With which ones can the congregation be most helpful?

3. Read **1 Corinthians 12:12-31** on spiritual gifts. If your church utilizes a spiritual gifts system, share the experiences you have had with it. Why is it unrealistic to expect the pastor or any other person to possess all the gifts needed by the church? What are the particular gifts that your pastor has? What gifts are present within your group or class?

4. Page 23 has a "Personal Development Inventory for Clergy." Visit with your pastor about the inventory. What items should be added to it? Are there any that you would remove? What items relate just as much to church members as to the pastor? How can the church help the pastor in personal development?

5. Pages 24-25 talk about bivocational clergy, who have become increasingly common in smaller congregations. What benefits does a church receive if it has a bivocational pastor? How could a congregation help a bivocational pastor be successful? If your church has a bivocational pastor, talk about the experiences you've had. While bivocational pastors are especially thought of in relationship to small congregations, they can also be part-time staff in very large congregations. Would your church consider a bivocational pastor in the future?

Session Three: *Taking Care of the Pastor* [pages 26-37]
1. Do the exercise "What's Most Important?" on page 28. Share results with others and talk about them. Involve the pastor if possible.
2. How do you feel about the "Four for One Rule" on page 31? One pastor said: "The church I serve has 325 members, and 275 of them see themselves as my boss. They all give me feedback." How would you feel if in that pastor's situation? Why is positive feedback very important? Under what circumstances does negative feedback or criticism become important?
3. Pages 33-34 speak about dealing with overly critical or antagonistic members. What causes people to function like this? What are the problems for the pastor and other staff confronting such people alone? How can church leaders help? How can the congregation avoid empowering people who are antagonistic?
4. Pages 35-36 discuss the expectations of pastoral spouses and children. What, perhaps unspoken, assumptions exist in your church concerning the pastor's spouse and children? How can church leaders and the congregation as a whole be supportive to the minister and his or her spouse?
5. Read **Luke 10:25-28**. How would the church treat the pastor if it took these words seriously?

Strengthening Pastoral Ministry

Session Four: *The Congregation–Supporting and Encouraging the Pastor* [pages 38–47]
1. Contrast the pastor's work with your own and with others in the congregation. What are the similarities? The differences? Why is the support of the congregation so important if the pastor is to be both healthy and effective?
2. Page 42 shares the fact that 90% of most church members feel reaching new people is important but that only 34% think outreach to the unchurched is as important in the pastor's use of time as ministry to members. Would that be the case in your church? Why, or why not?
3. How genuinely open to change is your congregation? How are differences of opinion handled in your church? Do you think the pastor of your church receives the support needed to work for change? Why, or why not? Visit with the pastor about this if possible.
4. Pages 45–46 talk about the challenge of viewing issues and concerns as a Christian rather than from the perspective of a consumer society. Talk about the bullet points. Read **1 Corinthians 13:1–13** and talk about the implications of those familiar words for the life of the church.
5. Pages 46–47 discuss spiritual gifts. What are the ministries to which you feel called in your church? In your home, at work, and in the community? How can the pastor best help people develop their own spiritual gifts and ministries in Christ's name?

Session Five: *When Change Comes* [pages 48–52]
1. Look at the list of reasons that can cause a pastor to move on page 48. Which of those have happened in your church? Which situations are most difficult?
2. There are some churches which want to grow but do not want a pastor to take strong leadership. What problems will a pastor have if he or she tries to demonstrate strong leadership in such a church? What problems will come to a pastor of such a church who does not take initiative? Why is it important for the style and gifts of the pastor to be compatible with the nature and needs of the congregation?
3. Read **Philippians 3:12–17**. What do these words suggest for churches going through pastoral transitions? How can the pastor and the church learn from the past without being held back by it?
4. What are the consequences if a pastor and a church are not open and honest with one another about issues of ministry? How are transitions helped when people are open and honest?
5. Share reflections on the last two pastoral changes in your church. What was done well? What could have been done better?

Where to Learn More

Clapp, Steve and Cindy Hollenberg, **Creating Quality in Ministry** (Andrew Center/LifeQuest, 1995, 1997].
Includes an expansion of the suggestions for pastors offered in this booklet.

Clapp, Steve, Ron Finney, and Angela Zizak, **Preaching, Planning, and Plumbing** [Christian Community, 1999].
Includes a spiritual gifts process and a discussion of bivocational ministry.

Coyner, Michael J. and Lyle E. Schaller, **Making a Good Move: Opening the Door to a Successful Pastorate** [Abingdon, 1999]. *A wonderful guide to new pastorates.*

Hybels, Bill, **Too Busy Not to Pray** [InterVarsity Press, 1988].

The LifeQuest Congregational Profile (LifeQuest/New Life Ministries, 2000, 2001, 2002]. *Comprehensive self-study.*

Mundey, Paul, **Change and the Established Congregation** [Andrew Center, 1994]. *Results of a study on change.*

Nouwen, Henri J.M., **In the Name of Jesus–Reflections on Christian Leadership** [Crossroad, 1989].

Oswald, Roy M. and Otto Kroeger, **Personality Type and Religious Leadership** [Alban Institute, 1988].

Schaller, Lyle E., **21 Bridges to the 21st Century–The Future of Pastoral Leadership** [Abingdon, 1994]. *Insightful and thought-provoking!*

Schaller, Lyle E., **44 Questions for Congregational Self-Appraisal** [Abingdon, 1998]. *A guide to churches seeking greater self-understanding.*

Schaller, Lyle E., **The Pastor and the People** [Abingdon, 1986]. *Though written several years ago, this book offers a wealth of practical strategies and helpful perspectives.*

Schaller, Lyle E., **The Very Large Church** [Abingdon, 2000]. *Helpful for understanding staffing issues in large churches.*

Schwarz, Christian, **Paradigm Shift in the Church** [ChurchSmart, 1999].

Simon, Sidney, **Negative Criticism** [Argus, 1988].

Swindoll, Chuck, **Strengthening Your Grip** [Word, 1982].

Wardle, Terry, **The Soul's Journey** [Sandberg Leadership Center, 2000]. *Illuminating!*